Dallas
iconography

Dallas
iconography

barry b. doyle

photographs of dallas

PELICAN PUBLISHING COMPANY
GRETNA 2009

Copyright © 2009
By Barry B. Doyle
All rights reserved

The word "Pelican" and the depiction of a pelican are trademarks of Pelican Publishing Company, Inc., and are registered in the U.S. Patent and Trademark Office.

Library of Congress Cataloging-in-Publication Data

Doyle, Barry B.
Dallas iconography / Barry B. Doyle
p. cm.
ISBN 9781589807020
1. Dallas—Photography. 2. U.S. cities—Dallas. I. Doyle, Barry B. II. Title.
   2008901315

Set in Adobe Myriad MM and Adobe Nueva MM
Book design by Barry B. Doyle

Printed in Singapore
Published by Pelican Publishing Company, Inc.
1000 Burmaster Street, Gretna, Louisiana 70053

table of contents

cityscapes	11
artscapes	29
zooscapes	43
fairscapes	49
floralscapes	55
map	60
notes & map key	61

Welcome to Dallas

Greetings!

On behalf of the City of Dallas and the Dallas Convention & Visitors Bureau, I am pleased to present *Dallas Iconography*, a compelling testament to the top destination in Texas. This striking compilation of photographs celebrates our city's multi-faceted and diverse urban landscape, arts and culture, architecture and attractions.

In Dallas, we *Live Large and Think Big*. This attractive book catalogs some ways our city lives up to this motto. To name a few, Dallas:

- Displays proudly its more than 300 public art works throughout the city and has the largest contiguous urban arts district in the nation—the Dallas Museum of Art, The Crow Collection of Asian Art, Nasher Sculpture Center and Morton H. Meyerson Symphony Center.

- Showcases buildings designed by this century's premier architects: I.M. Pei's Morton H. Meyerson Symphony Center and Dallas City Hall, Philip Johnson's John F. Kennedy Memorial and Renzo Piano's Nasher Sculpture Center.

- Offers the best shopping in the Southwest – NorthPark Center, Galleria, West Village, Victory Park, Highland Park Village and Mockingbird Station.

- Boasts many four- and five-diamond/star restaurants with world-class chefs, unique local restaurants showcasing regional favorites, plus Tex-Mex and barbecue.

Dallas Iconography makes a clear statement about our dynamic city. If you're not from around here, we think flipping these pages will make you want to experience Dallas. So come see us and find out why Dallas continues to reign as the #1 visitor destination in Texas.

Sincerely,

Phillip J. Jones
President/CEO
Dallas Convention & Visitors Bureau
www.dallascvb.com

Acknowledgments

There's always a backstory. There's always a motivation and an inspiration. I'd like to thank my long suffering and eminently supportive bride and partner for these past 26 years. Without Eve's help, guidance and management, this modest compilation would not have come about. She's the best person I know and the best thing that ever happened to me. Thanks, dear.

I'd like to thank those that offered critical suggestions and support, part of a far flung creative community of friends committed to mutual nourishment and fun. Janine Roach, Matt and Kimberly A. Schmitt, Petra and Chris Rowell, Bill Schwartz, Leah Turner and Devena Karpelman all provided help and encouragement. Thanks also to Chris Hannon, the nicest person I know, for technical assistance, time and again. I am in debt to my good friend Tom Gallagher for his professional advice, the best copyright and patent lawyer on the East Coast. Lastly, thanks go to Karen Peterson for her invaluable editing assistance and suggestions.

Let's see, in order that's LA; Denver; Newbury Park, CA; Waterbury, Vermont; Nottinghamshire, UK; Seattle; Ontario, Canada; Stamford, Connecticut and Dallas. Thank the stars for the Internet.

This book is dedicated to Eve, Colin, Tory and Evan—the real stars in my firmament.

A Technical Note

The book was put together using elements of Adobe Creative Suite 3; Adobe InDesign, Photoshop, Illustrator and Acrobat. I also use Apple's Aperture, a professional photo storage and management application. Layout and pre-production were done on a Powermac G5 with twin 23" displays.

The images are divided by theme into chapters. There is an annotated appendix showing selected images and links to websites if applicable. Also included is a reference map noting interesting sites, transportation information and the locations where the photographs were taken.

The camera used is a Nikon D200 digital SLR camera with a variety of prime and zoom lenses.

cityscapes

images from around the city

above
Completed in 1892, the Old Red Courthouse has undergone extensive renovations

right
The interior of "Old Red" was carefully and meticulously restored

above
The JFK Memorial Plaza designed by architect Phillip Johnson

right
Inside the cenotaph lies a black granite square inscribed with the President's name

above
The grassy knoll at Dealey Plaza

right
View from near Texas School Book Depository across Dealey Plaza to the Hyatt Regency and Reunion Tower.

next page
The Depository is now known as the Dallas County Administration Building. Count up from the ground floor level on the right side for the infamous sixth floor window, framed by the tree loop.

previous page top
A view from south of the Trinity River near the appropriately named Townview Center. The campus houses six magnet high schools including two of the top rated schools in the nation—The Talented and Gifted High School and The Science and Engineering Magnet High School

previous page bottom
Fishing on the Trinity can produce channel catfish or just a good time on a warm afternoon

below
The Trinity River Project will transform the river bottom and levees into parkland and a tollway. Internationally acclaimed architect Santiago Calatrava has designed several bridges that will span the river

above
The courtyard at the aptly named Fountain Place, designed by I. M. Pei

right
Reflection of the top of Fountain Place in the façade of Renaissance Tower

next page
Fountain Place viewed from the south

previous page
The Glory Window inside the spiral-shaped Chapel of Thanksgiving attracts thousands of visitors each year. The window was designed by French artist Gabriel Loire

below
The Thanksgiving Tower lies just south of Thanksgiving Square. The Chapel shown at lower left was designed by noted architect Phillip Johnson

right
The Golden Rule mosaic at Thanksgiving Square after the painting by Norman Rockwell by the Cavallini Company

above
Victory Plaza at American Airlines Center arena, home of the Dallas Mavericks and Dallas Stars

right
At the entry to Victory Plaza is the W Hotel. The glass bottomed balcony

Dallas City Hall is another of I.M.Pei's buildings. Shaped like an inverted triangular prism, it typifies Pei's angular, modernist style.

Quiet, peaceful neighborhoods provide oases from the sturm and drang of modern city life

And sometimes a rare quiet snow falls

From the sublime to the sublime. Spend the morning shopping at Highland Park Village, then mosey on over to Sonny Bryan's Original Smokehouse for an unforgettable barbeque lunch

The Gaylord Texan near DFW Airport is safe from the elements—encased in a protective dome. The hotel is part of the Gaylord Opryland Nashville Hotel group

right
The Mission Plaza in the Lone Star Atrium

artscapes

images of art and culture

Rush Hour, 1983
George Segal, 1924-2000
Nasher Sculpture Center

left
Walking to the Sky, 2004
Jonathan Borofsky 1942-
Nasher Sculpture Center

below
Working Model for Three Piece No. # Vertebrae, 1968
Henry Moore 1898-1986
Nasher Sculpture Center

bottom
Just east of downtown is Deep Ellum, a vibrant nightclub and bohemian area that boasts a variety of street art

Genesis, The Gift of Life, 1954
Miguel Covarrubias, 1904-57
Dallas Museum of Art

Hart Window, 1995
Dale Chihuly, 1941-
Dallas Museum of Art

next page
Cattle drive sculpture at Pioneer Plaza, 1992
Robert Summers, 1940-
adjacent to the Dallas Convention Center

20 Elements, 2005
Joel Shapiro, 1941-
NorthPark Center

Corridor Pin, Bleu, 1999
Claes Oldenburg, 1929-
and Coosje van Bruggen, 1942-
NorthPark Center

next page
Quantum Cloud XX (tornado), 2000
Antony Gormley, 1950-
Nasher Sculpture Center

The Morton H. Meyerson Symphony Center is in the heart of the Arts District. The Meyerson is home to the world-class Dallas Symphony Orchestra and other cultural organizations like the Turtle Creek Chorale, the Dallas Wind Symphony and the Greater Dallas Youth Orchestra

above and next page
The Mustangs of Las Colinas, 1984
Robert Glen, 1940-
Williams Square, Las Colinas, Irving

zooscapes

images from the Dallas Zoo

left to right

Mandrill
Mandrillus sphinx

Chimpanzee
Pan troglodytes

Meerkat
Suricata suricatta

Western lowland gorilla
Gorilla gorilla gorilla

previous page clockwise from top
Cuckoo
Guira guira

Grey-headed kingfisher
Halcyon leucocephala

The chicken-sized Crown Victoria Pigeon
Goura victoria

above and left
Western Lowland Gorilla
Gorilla gorilla gorilla

African elephant
Loxodonta africana
front and back

Reticulated giraffe
Giraffa camelopardalis reticulata

Hilde, facing right, and her daughter in a pushmi-pullyu pose. She was the oldest giraffe in the world when she died at 33 in 2007. Zoos across the country are populated with her offspring.

  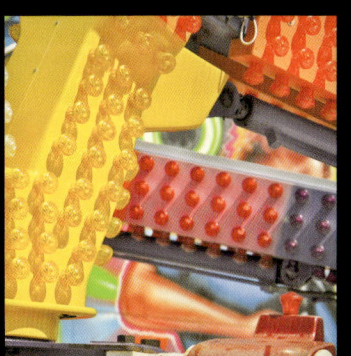 

fairscapes

images from the State Fair of Texas

left to right

Big Tex welcome

The Texas Star

Midway lights

Big Tex backside

top
A view from the Texas Skyway gondola ride that traverses the fairgrounds

above
Deep fried guacamole

right
Cholester-what?

above
The Texas Star, North America's largest Ferris wheel as seen from the Midway

right
Everyone needs an authentic Fletcher's Corny Dog

following pages
More scenes from the Midway

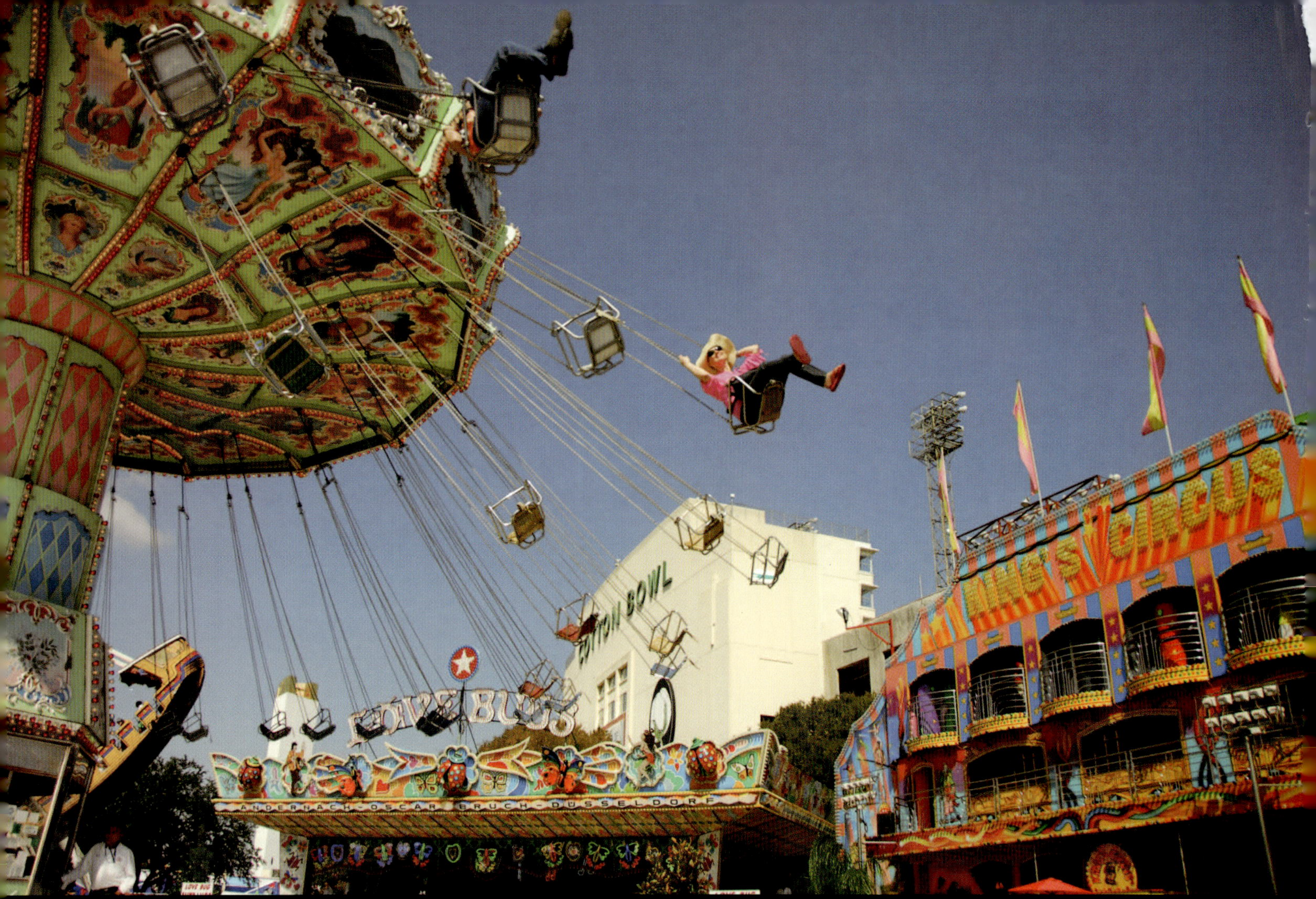

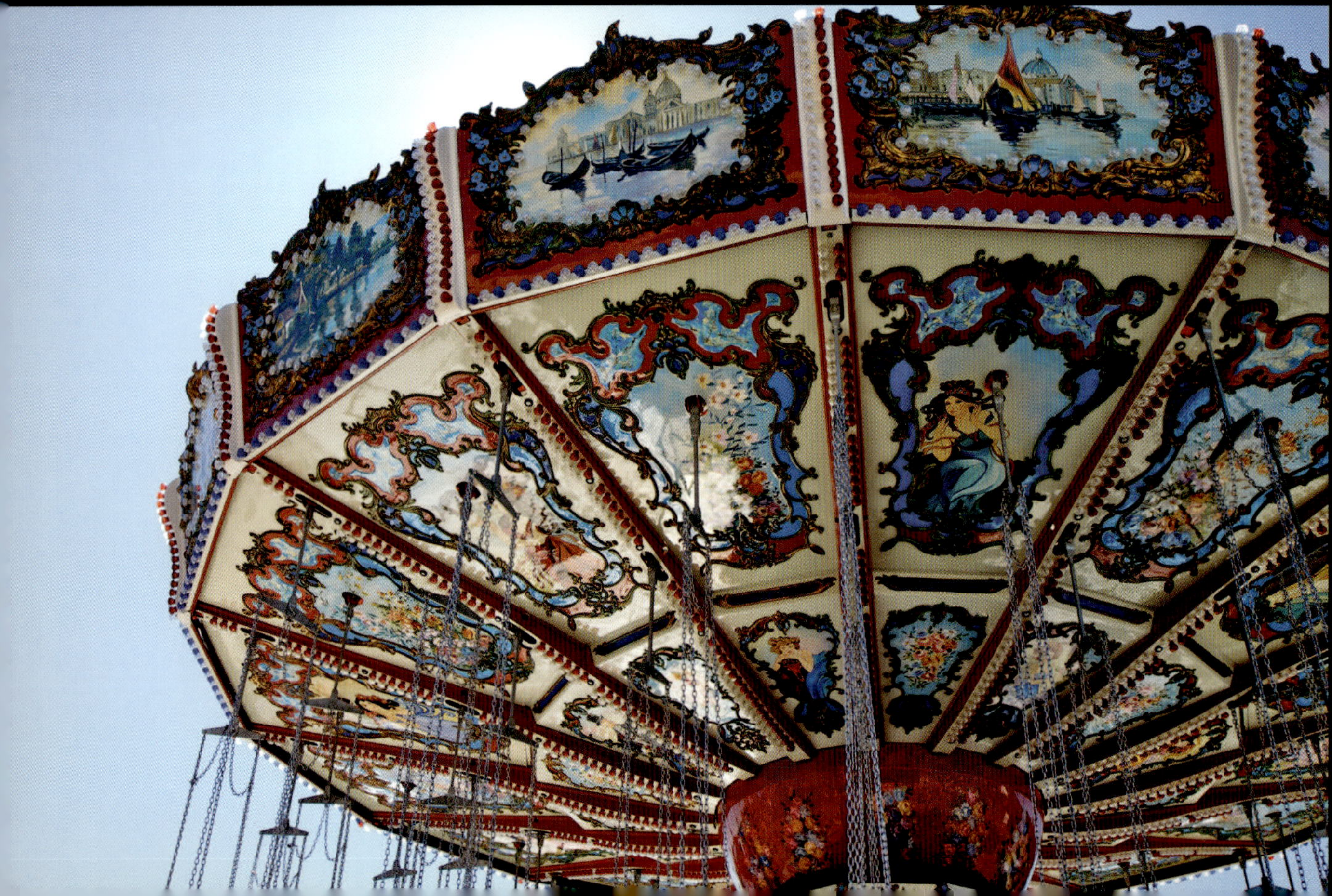

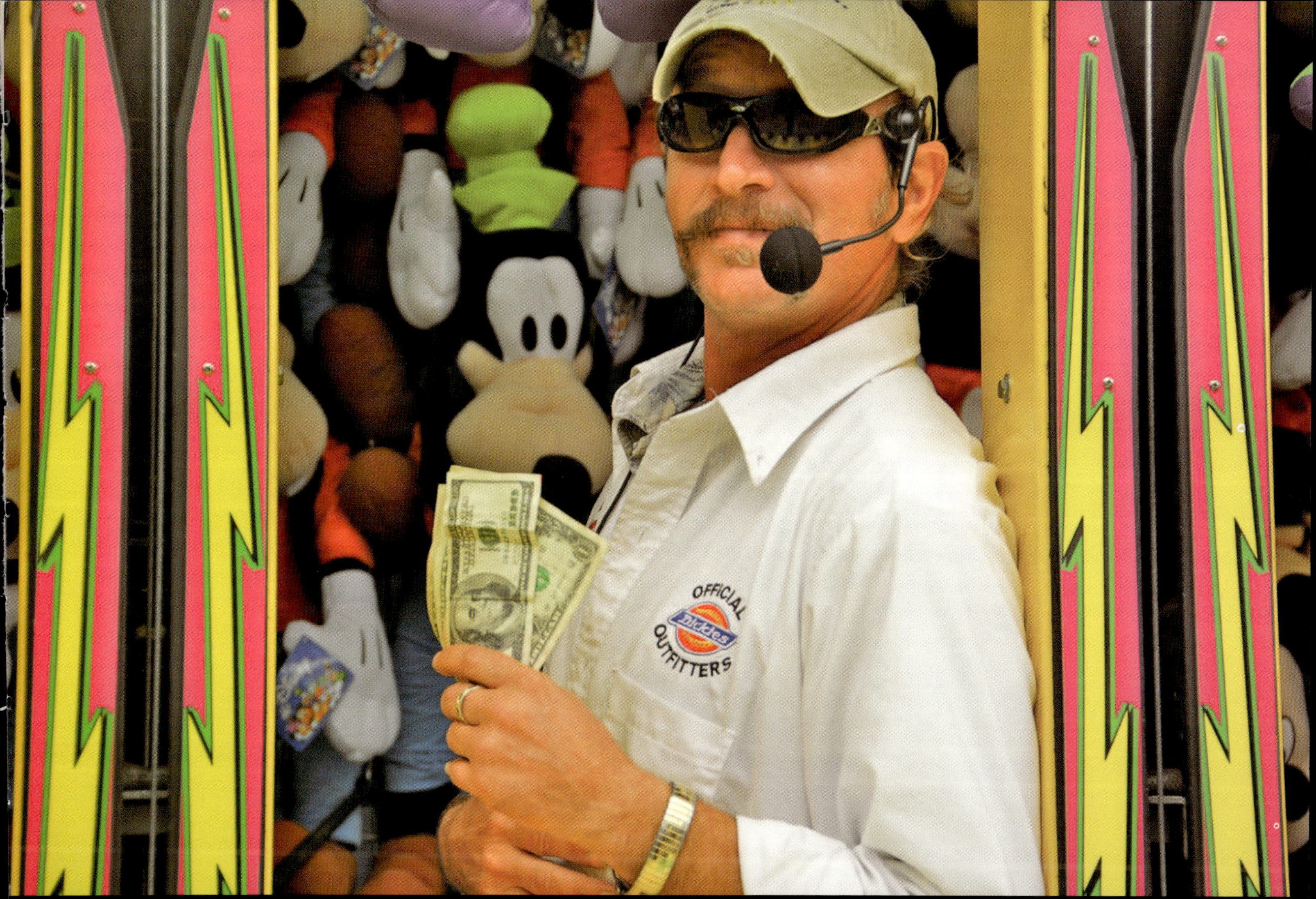
OFFICIAL
Dickies
OUTFITTERS

WIN BIG

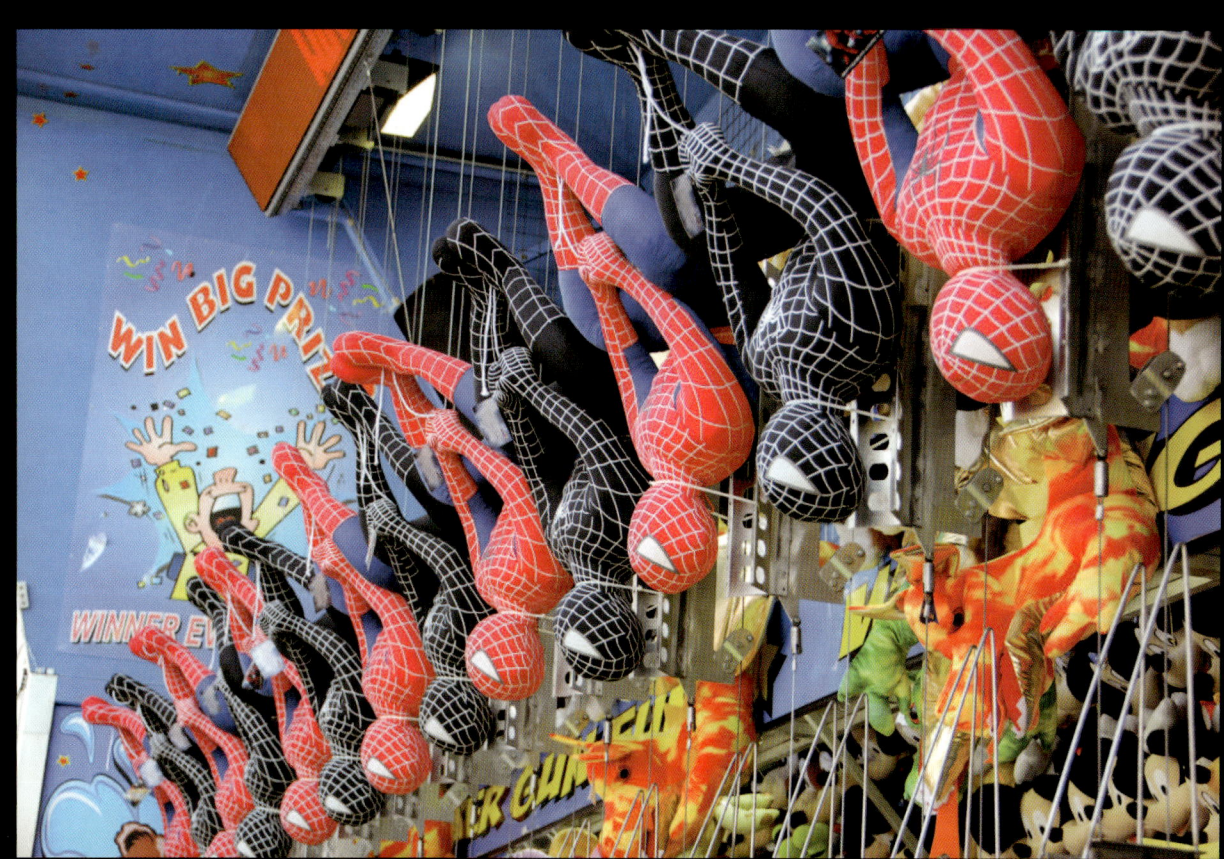

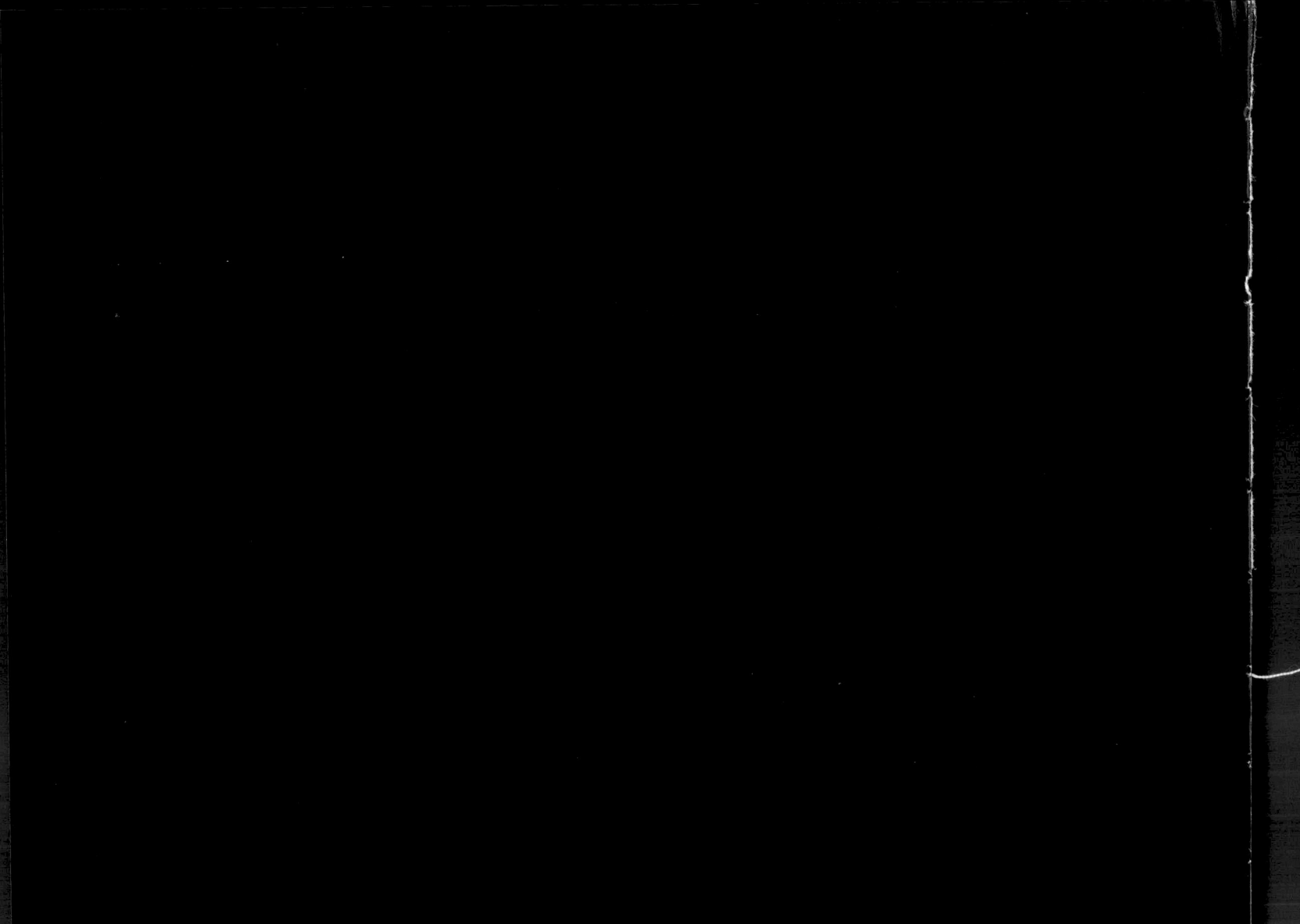

floralscapes

images from and near the Dallas Arboretum

top and right
Rancho Encinal, with views of White Rock Lake and the Dallas skyline, was the estate of petroleum entrepreneur Everrette DeGolyer. It is now a part of the Dallas Arboretum

above
Heavenly Bamboo, *Nana nandina*, is a local favorite and graces the DeGolyer homestead

A study in contrasts—tulips come early to Dallas and thrive in the spring rain. Crape Myrtles, *Largerstoemia indica,* do very well in the sere, hot summers. They provide color mid-year with blossoms of various hues and in the fall with subtle leaf colors

One can enjoy a cool shady spot below the White Rock Lake spillway, just west of the Dallas Arboretum. White Rock Lake in East Dallas provides a haven year round for biking, hiking, running, walking and sailing. The view here is to the south near Mockingbird Lane

next page
Spider lily
Lycoris radiata

1 1700 Pacific/DART Store	13 Dallas Museum of Art	25 Greyhound Terminal	37 Renaissance Tower
2 2001 Bryan Tower	14 Dallas Public Library	26 Hampton Inn	38 San Jacinto Tower
3 2100 McKinney	15 Dallas World Aquarium	27 Holiday Inn-Aristocrat Hotel	39 Sixth Floor Museum
4 Adam's Mark Hotel	16 DART Headquarters	28 Hyatt Regency Dallas Hotel	40 A. Maceo Smith Federal Bldg
5 Adolphus Hotel	17 Earl Cabell Federal Building	29 Lincoln Plaza	41 Southwestern Bell Plaza
6 Bank of America Building	18 El Centro College	30 Magestic Theater	42 Thanksgiving Square
7 Bank One Tower	19 Fairmont Hotel	31 Maxus Energy Tower	43 Thanksgiving Tower
8 Belo Mansion	20 Federal Reserve Bank of Dallas	32 Meyerson Symphony Center	44 Trammell Crow Center
9 Cathedral Guadalupe	21 First Baptist Church	33 Neiman Marcus	45 US Post Office
10 Chase Tower	22 Fountain Place Tower	34 One Dallas Center	46 Woodall Rodgers Tower
11 Crescent Court	23 Magnolia Hotel	35 One Main Place	47 YMCA Building
12 Dallas Education Center	24 Grand Hotel	36 Plaza of the Americas	48 Nasher Sculpture Center

Notes and Map Key

Photo locations on the map page

1 *Cover Back, pp. 4, 5, 30, 40, 41*
The Latino Cultural Center was designed by architect Ricardo Legorreta. The site features an art gallery and sculpture courtyards.

www.dallasculture.org/latinoCulturalCenter.cfm

2 *Cover Front*
This Pegasus sat atop a Mobil gas station in Casa Linda for 50 years. Before that it was displayed at the 1939 World's Fair in New York City.
www.oldred.org

3 *Pages 2, 64*
Big Tex has welcomed State Fair-goers since 1952. Tex is 52 feet tall, wears size 70 boots, a 75 gallon hat and huge pair of Lee jeans.

www.bigtex.com

5 *Pages 6, 11, 16*
Hyatt Reunion Tower rises 55 stories affording a 360° view from the observation deck. Above the deck Antares restaurant completes a rotation every 55 minutes.
www.dallasregency.hyatt.com

Page 8
The author's beautiful bride and the inspiration for the book. Eve Becker-Doyle is the CEO of the National Athletic Trainers' Association based in Dallas, Texas.
www.nata.org

6 *Page 11*
Dallas is known for its wonderful restaurants, from casual to 5 star. They say you should never order a margarita unless you're in a border state, but that doesn't apply in Dallas.

7 *Page 12*
Construction on the Old Red Courthouse began in 1890. In 1919 the original clocktower was removed when prevailing winds threatened its stability.
www.oldred.org

8 *Page 13*
A cenotaph is a sepulchral monument erected in memory of a deceased person whose body is buried elsewhere.
www.jfk.org/Research/Kennedy_Memorial/Contents.htm

4 *Page 14*
The grassy knoll at Dealey Plaza is one of Dallas' most frequented destinations for visitors and locals alike.

www.jfk.org

7 *Pages 14, 15*
The Sixth Floor Museum at the old Texas School Book Depository is an iconic symbol of Dallas. Don't forget to visit the seventh floor for the current exhibit.
www.jfk.org

9 *Pages 16, 17*
The Trinity River has had an unusual history. Navigable to Dallas in the 19th century, it will now have a tollway between the levees, the first such roadway in the nation.
www.trinityrivercorridor.com/

10 *Pages 18, 19*
Fountain Place, 1445 Ross Avenue, is west of the Arts District, and north of the Central Business District.

www.fountainplace.com

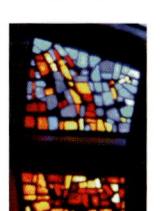

11 *Pages 20, 21*
One of the largest horizontally mounted stained-glass pieces in the world, the Glory Window forms the 60-foot-high ceiling of the Chapel of Thanksgiving.
www.thanksgiving.org/window

12 *Page 22*
The American Airlines Center was designed by David M. Schwarz/Architectural Services, and HKS. It is home to the Mavericks, Stars and Desperados and hosts numerous concerts.
www.americanairlinescenter.com

13 *Page 23*
The Dallas City Hall plaza features an oversized bronze sculpture by Henry Moore appropriately named *The Dallas Piece*.

www.dallascityhall.com/html/dallas_city_hall

14 *Page 25*
This technique of selective focus is best produced with a tilt shift lens, but can be emulated in software such as Photoshop. A PS tutorial can be found here:
www.recedinghairline.co.uk/tutorials/fakemodel

(15) *Page 26*
Home of many of the area's rich and famous, Highland Park and University Park are two cities completely surrounded by the city of Dallas.
www.hpvillage.com

(16) *Page 27*
A tilt shift software emulation brings a singular element into enhanced focus as seen from a hotel balcony within the Gaylord Texas Resort.
www.gaylordhotels.com/gaylordtexan

(17) *Page 30*
The Nasher Sculpture Center is not just about art in a fabulous setting—the Italian travertine galleries feature an innovative aluminum sun screen providing beautiful light.
www.nashersculpturecenter.org

(17) *Page 31*
Found all over the world, Jonathan Borofsky's most famous works are his *Hammering Man* sculptures.

www.borofsky.com

(19) *Page 32*
The Dallas Museum of Art is one of only three cities to host a 7 month exhibition of the Treasures of Tutankhamen, an encore of its tour 30 years ago.
www.dallasmuseumofart.org

(20) *Page 33*
Adjacent to the Convention Center, the bronze cattle drive is located on the actual 1850s Shawnee Trail. It is the largest bronze monument of its kind in the world.
www.dallascvb.com/visitors

(21) *Page 34*
Northpark Center opened in 1965, the first large-scale mall to offer unity of architecture for the retailers and for the purpose of displaying modern art.
www.northparkcenter.com

(17) *Page 35*
To see more of Antony Gormley's work, visit *www.flickr.com/groups/gormley* and his personal web site: *www.antonygormley.com*

(22) *Pages 36*
A combination of overlapping geometric forms, the Morton H. Myerson Symphony Center represents another collaboration between the city of Dallas and architect I. M. Pei.
www.meyersonsymphonycenter.com

(23) *Page 37*
At the north end of downtown, a silent conductor overlooks the expanding heart of the Dallas Arts District. *The Storm* is a story of all the arts in a symphony of creativity.
www.eye-c.com

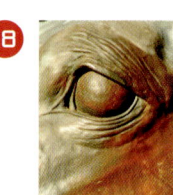
(18) *Pages 38, 39*
The Mustangs of Las Colinas is the largest equestrian sculpture in the world. A bronze installation of nine wild mustangs runs across a fabricated granite stream.
www.mustangsoflascolinas.com

(24) *Pages 43-47*
The Dallas Zoo has something for everyone, from gorillas and chimps to meerkats and tigers. Don't miss the monorail or forget to visit the Lacerte Children's Zoo.
www.dallaszoo.org

(24) *Page 45*
Plan to arrive just as the zoo opens. Patrick, the Western Lowland Gorilla may interact if you are respectful and quiet. There are two gorilla habitats—he's in the western one.

(3) *Pages 43-47*
The State Fair of Texas runs from late September to mid-October. The first State Fair at this location was held in 1886.

www.bigtex.com

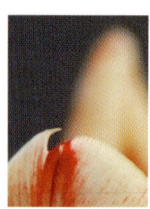
(25) *Page 45*
Located at 8525 Garland Road on the southeast side of White Rock Lake, the Dallas Arboretum maintains an amazing 2,800 species of azaleas in its collection.
www.dallasarboretum.org